MU01061309

In classes in the socia
you may be asked to t
tion) system for documenting sources. The guidelines in this booklet follow those set forth in the *Publication Manual of the American Psychological Association*, 7th edition (2020).

Even though the new guidelines present a system for citing many different kinds of sources, they may not cover every type of source you need to cite. At times you may find that you have to think critically to adapt the guidelines to the sources you are using.

Creating APA-style in-text citations

Directory to APA in-text citation models

APA style requires you to supply an in-text citation each time you quote, paraphrase, summarize, or otherwise integrate material from a source. In-text citations are made with a combination of signal phrases and parenthetical references and include the information needed to give credit and for readers to locate the full reference in the list of references at the end of the text.

When citing a source in your text, include the following in a signal phrase or parenthetical citation:

- the author's (or authors') last name(s)
- the year in which the source was published
- a page number or other section locator (for a direct quotation)

In APA style, a page number or other section locator need not be included for a summary or paraphrase, but check with your instructors to make sure you understand their requirements.

There is a direct connection between the in-text citation and the first part of the corresponding entry in the list of references. It is crucial that the name and year mentioned in the in-text citation match the name and year in the reference list. The reference list is alphabetized by authors' last names, and if there is a mistake in the list or in the in-text citation, readers won't easily be able to find the source they are looking for in the list of references.

SAMPLE IN-TEXT CITATION

Bruns (2017) argued that by imprisoning men—"which discourages shared responsibility for children, the home, and the household economy—prisons, jails, and justice system processes reproduce gender inequality" (p. 1332).

REFERENCE LIST ENTRY

Bruns, A. (2017). Consequences of partner incarceration for women's employment. *Journal of Marriage and Family, 79*(5), 1331–1352. https://doi.org/10.1111/jomf.12412

NOTE: APA style requires the use of the past tense or the present perfect tense in signal phrases introducing cited material: Smith (2020) reported; Smith (2020) has argued.

1. Basic format for a quotation   Ordinarily, introduce the quotation with a signal phrase (what the APA calls a "narrative citation") that includes the author's last name and the year of publication in parentheses. Include the page number in parentheses following the quotation.

Zhang (2019) showed that "when academics are strongly motivated to teach and are satisfied with and take pride in their teaching," their feeling of affiliation with the schools at which they teach increases (p. 1325).

If the author is not named in a signal phrase, include the author's surname, the year of publication, and the page number in parentheses following the quotation:

". . ." (Zhang, 2019, p. 1325).

2. Basic format for a summary or a paraphrase   As when citing a quotation (see item 1), include the author's last name and the year the work was published either before the borrowed material or in parentheses following it. A page number is not required for a summary or a paraphrase, but include one if it would help readers find the passage in a long work or if your instructor requires it.

> Instructors' positive feelings about teaching carry over into their feelings about the schools at which they teach (Zhang, 2019, p. 211).

3. Quotation from a source without page numbers   If your source does not include page numbers, include other information from the source—a section heading, a paragraph number, a figure or table number, a slide number, or a time stamp—to help readers find the cited passage:

> Lopez (2019) has noted that ". . ." (Symptoms section).
>
> Myers (2019) extolled the benefits of humility (para. 5).
>
> Brezinski and Zhang (2017) traced the increase . . . (Figure 3).
>
> The American Immigration Council has recommended that ". . ." (Slide 5).
>
> In a recent TED Talk, Gould (2019) argued that ". . ." (13:27).

Do not include location numbers for sources in e-book format. If you shorten a lengthy heading, place it in quotation marks: ("What Is It" section).

4. Specific section of a source   To cite a specific section of a source, such as a portion of an audio or video recording; a slide in a set of lecture slides; or a dedication, preface, foreword, afterword, or chapter, name the section in your in-text citation.

> In a dedication written while he was in hiding, Salman Rushdie (1991) included an acrostic of his son's name: SAFAR.

If the section was written by someone other than the author, include the section author's name in your in-text citation.

> In his foreword to Anthony Ray Hinton's moving book (2018), Bryan Stevenson wrote . . . (p. iv).

In your reference list, include a citation for the work as a whole.

5. Two authors Name both authors in a signal phrase or in the parenthetical citation. In the parenthetical citation, use an ampersand (&) between the authors' names; in the signal phrase, use the word "and."

> Bloomberg and Pope (2017) have argued that with global warming we are facing a "*kairos*: a supreme moment at which one simply must act, however implausible or inconvenient" (p. 12).

> Some have argued that we are facing a watershed moment, or "*kairos,*" in the fight against global warming (Bloomberg & Pope, 2017, p. 12).

6. Three or more authors Use the first author's name followed by "et al." (Latin for "and others") in either a signal phrase or a parenthetical citation.

> Similarly, as Belenky et al. (1986) showed, examining the lives of women expands our understanding of human development.

> Examining the lives of women expands our understanding of human development (Belenky et al., 1986).

7. Organization as author If the author is a government agency or some other organization, give the group's full name in a signal phrase or parenthetical citation the first time you cite the source.

> The Kaiser Family Foundation (2018) found that 11% of children living in Texas were uninsured in 2017.

> In 2017, 11% of children living in Texas were uninsured (Kaiser Family Foundation, 2018).

For an organization with a lengthy name, you may abbreviate the name of the organization in citations after the first. Include the abbreviation—in parentheses in the signal phrase or in brackets in the parenthetical citation—following the organization's full name.

FIRST CITATION   The Centers for Disease Control and Prevention (CDC, 2019) found that . . .
or
(Centers for Disease Control and Prevention [CDC], 2019)

LATER CITATIONS   (CDC, 2019)

For a work by a government agency or large organization with multiple, nested departments, list the most specific agency or department as the author, as in the reference list (see item 5, p. 16).

8. Unknown or anonymous author If the author is unknown, include the work's title (shortened if lengthy) in the in-text citation.

> As a result of changes in the city's eviction laws, New York's eviction rate dropped by over a third from 2013 to 2018 ("Pushed Out," 2019).

All titles in in-text citations are set in title case: Capitalize the first and last words of a title and subtitle, all significant words, and any words of four letters or more. For books and most stand-alone works (except websites), italicize the title; for most articles and other parts of larger works, set the title in quotation marks.

Only in rare cases, when "Anonymous" is specified as the author, use the word "Anonymous" in the author position: (Anonymous, 2020). (Also use the word "Anonymous" at the start of the reference list entry.)

NOTE: Titles are treated differently in reference list entries. See the "Title" and "Source" sections of "Elements of APA reference list entries" on pages 10–12.

9. Two or more works by the same author in the same year In your reference list, use lowercase letters ("a," "b," and so on) with the year to order the entries. Use the same letter in your in-text citation. (See item 13 in the reference list section, p. 17.)

> Soot-free flames can be produced by stripping the air of nitrogen and then adding that nitrogen to the fuel (Conover, 2019b).

10. Two or more authors with the same last name To avoid confusion, use the authors' initials in the in-text references.

> K. Yi (2019) has demonstrated . . .
>
> D. Yi (2017) has shown that . . .

If the authors share the same initials, spell out each author's first name:

> Kim Yi (2019) has demonstrated . . .
>
> Kenneth Yi (2017) has shown that . . .

11. Indirect source (source quoted in another source)   Best practice is to find and use the original source. If that is not possible (for example, if the source has not been translated), cite the original source and then include "as cited in" plus the author's name and the date of the secondary source.

> One reviewer commended the author's "sure understanding of the thoughts of young people" (Brailsford, 1990, as cited in Chow, 2019, para. 9).

If you mention the original author in a signal phrase, just include "as cited in" plus the secondary source in the parenthetical citation.

12. Two or more works in the same parentheses   When your parenthetical citation names two or more works, put the citations in alphabetical order, separated by semicolons.

> So far, studies of pharmacological treatments for childhood obesity have been inconclusive (Barbour et al., 2018; Xu & Xue, 2016).

13. Work available in multiple versions   Some works may be available in more than one version. For example, an article may be reprinted in a collection or anthology, an older work may have been republished, or a translated work may be available in both the original language and other languages. If you consulted a reprinted, republished, or translated work, include both the date of original publication and the date of the version you used, and separate the dates with a slash: (Padura, 2009/2014).

14. Sacred or classical text   For a religious work (such as the Bible, the Torah, or the Qur'an), include the title of the version you consulted, the year of that version's publication, and the chapter, verse, and line numbers.

> (*New International Version Bible,* 1978/2011, Proverbs 16:18).

For a classic of poetry or drama, provide the author, year (or years) of publication, and the relevant numbered sections: For poetry, use canto, book, or other section names or numbers, and line numbers; for plays, use act, scene, and line numbers.

(Milton, 1667/2017, 1.263)

(Shakespeare, 1595/2010, 1.1.134)

See also item 35, "Sacred or classical text," in the reference list section (p. 24).

15. Website, software, or app   Most references to digital works or works published online can be cited in the text of your paper using one of the models shown previously in this section:

- If author and publication date are supplied, use the usual author-date format: (Smith, 2019).
- If the reference list entry uses "n.d." ("no date"), use that in your in-text citation: (Smith, n.d.). See pages 9–10.
- If the source is listed by the organization's name in the reference list, use the organization as author: (Greenpeace, 2019).

Whichever format you use, be sure that your in-text citation matches what you have used in your reference list entry. For example, if you quote, paraphrase, or summarize a tweet, include either the actual name or the screen name of the author in your text, depending on what appears in the author position in your reference list. (See item 62 in the reference list section, p. 32.)

However, if you merely refer to a website, a type of software, or an app in your text without citing specific information from that work, then no formal in-text citation (or reference list entry) is needed. Just mention the work, and include the URL.

16. Audiovisual or multimedia works   In the "author" position, include the name of the person (or people) primarily responsible for producing the work and the date it was created or released. For example, to cite a work in a museum, include the artist's name and the date the work was created: (O'Keeffe, 1931).

To cite a film, include the director's name and the date the film was released: (Hitchcock, 1959).

See the "Author" section (p. 9) in "Elements of APA reference list entries" and the introductory portion of "Multimedia sources" (p. 26) for more about whom to include in the "author" position.

17. Personal communications   Personal communications include a variety of source types, from text messages and emails you received to interviews and oral histories you recorded and live classes you attended. Cite personal communications that cannot be accessed by your readers in the text only; they should not be included in the list of references.

> A researcher studying the effect of the media on children's eating habits has argued that advertisers for snack foods should be required to design ads responsibly for their younger viewers (F. Johnson, personal communication, October 20, 2019).

Include any other information in the text that readers would need to understand the reference, such as the tribal membership for oral traditions.

Creating APA-style reference list entries

For an APA-style research project, you will develop a "References" list, an alphabetical list of the works you cite throughout your project. Place the list of references at the end of your paper or project. For advice on preparing the reference list, see "Formatting student papers in APA style" (p. 33). For a sample reference list, see page 43.

Elements of APA reference list entries

An APA-style reference consists of four parts:

- The **author**'s (or authors') name(s)
- The **date** of publication
- The **title** of the work
- The **source** of the work (the retrieval information)

Insert a period following each of these four parts.

author	date	title

Gazzaniga, M. S. (2019). *The consciousness instinct: Unraveling the mystery of how the*

source information

brain makes the mind. Farrar, Straus and Giroux.

In general, the first two elements—author and date of publication—appear in both in-text citations and reference list entries. In general, the title and source information appear only in the reference list entry.

Author

The author is the person or people most responsible for the work:

- For a book or article, the author is the person (or people) who wrote it.
- For a movie, the person most responsible is the director.
- For a government report, the author might be the specific agency that produced the report.
- For a company's annual report, the author is probably the corporation that produced the report.

If the role of the individual who produced the work is not that of author, include a brief description in parentheses identifying the role, such as "Ed." for "Editor." (For more about listing authors, see "General guidelines for listing authors," p. 14.)

Date of publication

In the in-text citation, the date of publication is the year the item appeared; in the reference list entry, the date may be the year alone, or it may be more specific:

- For a daily newspaper, weekly magazine, podcast episode, or blog or social media post, include the year, month, and day: (2019, February 10).
- For a monthly magazine, include the year and month: (2019, May).
- For a book or scholarly journal, include the year: (2019).
- For a multivolume work or TV series, include a range of years: (2011–2019).

For some works—such as a translation or a work that was reprinted in another source or republished at a later date—you may need to supply two dates. (See item 34, p. 24) If the reference list uses "(n.d.)" ("no date"), include "(n.d.)" in your in-text citation.

Title

The title is the name of the specific part of the work you consulted. This can be a bit tricky to determine, so it may help to consider whether the work is

- a stand-alone item, such as a novel, a website, a movie, a one-time TV special (such as the 2019 Grammy Awards), or a one-off podcast, *or*
- part of a larger whole, such as an article in a journal, a chapter in a book, a web page on a website, or an episode in a weekly podcast or TV series.

If the item you consulted is a separate work, then your title is just the title of that work. Set it in italics. Type the titles of stand-alone works in sentence case (capitalize only the first word of the title and subtitle and any proper nouns):

Culture code: The secrets of highly successful groups.

Out east: Memoir of a Montauk summer.

If the item you consulted is part of a larger whole, then set the title of the part you consulted in regular font (without quotation marks or italics), in sentence case:

Why we believe in conspiracy theories.

Robert Caro reflects on Robert Moses, L.B.J., and his own career in nonfiction.

If you are citing a nonacademic source or one that is not peer-reviewed (such as a newsletter or press release), or if you think the type of source you are citing will not be clear to your readers, include a bracketed label (like "[Newsletter]" or "[Video]") following the title.

Once upon a time . . . in Hollywood [Film].

Source

The source section of a reference entry supplies the information readers need to identify and locate the source:

- For a stand-alone work, like a book, the source information is the publication information: the publisher and, if the work was accessed online, a DOI (or digital object identifier) or direct-link URL.
- For a work that is part of a larger work, such as an article in a journal or a chapter in a collection or an edited book, the source information is information about the larger work, such as the publisher (for a book) and the volume, issue, and page numbers and a DOI or URL (for a journal article).

Source title   Titles of periodicals and books are set in italics; the names of websites are set in regular font. Periodical titles (journals, magazines, newspapers) and website names are set in title case (capitalize all words of four or more letters and all significant words):

> *Journal of Applied Psychology.*
>
> *The Wall Street Journal.*

Book titles are set in sentence case (capitalize the first word of the title and subtitle and any proper nouns):

> *The Oxford encyclopedia of psychology and aging.*

Publisher (for books)   For books, include the full name of the publisher following the title. Omit terms that indicate corporate structure, like "Inc." or "Ltd.," but otherwise set the publisher's name as it appears on the book itself. (The publisher's location is not included.)

Volume and issue number (for periodicals)   Scholarly journals and some magazines are published in "volumes" (all the issues published in a single year) and "issues" (the periodical published each week, month, or quarter). If available, include volume and issue numbers after the periodical's title. (Newspapers and many magazines are published simply by date.) Volume numbers are italicized; issue numbers (which appear in parentheses) are not: *12*(3).

Page numbers For a selection that appears in a book, include the page number(s) for the part you consulted following the collection or anthology title, after the abbreviation "p." (for "page") or "pp." (for "pages"; see item 19, p. 20). For an article that appears in a periodical, include the page numbers (with no "p." or "pp.") after the issue number, or after the periodical's title if no volume or issue number is available. (See items 14, 15, and 16, pp. 18–19.)

DOIs and URLs If a digital object identifier (DOI) is available, include it at the end of the citation with no period at the end. If there is no DOI but you can supply a direct-link URL, do so; if not, omit the URL. If the DOI or URL is lengthy, you can include a shortened form by using a site like shortdoi.org or bitly.com. Some sites (like that of *The New York Times*) provide shortened permalinks.

Include the DOI as a link. The APA recommends using the International DOI Foundation's current format.

https://doi.org/10.1037/apl0000377

If you encounter a DOI in a different format, change the beginning to "https://doi.org/" and add the DOI number for the specific work (with no space between the slash and the DOI).

Now let's put this all together and look at a couple of examples of reference entries.

If you read an article in a journal, your reference entry consists of the author's name, the article's title, and information about the source (the journal in which the article appeared):

REFERENCE LIST ENTRY FOR AN ARTICLE IN A JOURNAL

author	(date)	title	source title	*volume* (issue)	pages
Becker, G. S.	(1995).	The economics of crime.	*Cross Sections,*	*12*(3),	8–15.

However, if you read the same article in a collection of essays, then the author and title remain the same, but the source section now includes information about the collection in which the article appeared. Information about the original publication appears at the end of the citation.

REFERENCE LIST ENTRY FOR AN ARTICLE FROM A COLLECTION

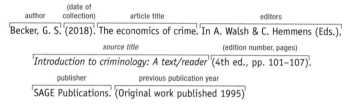

If you can't find all the information you need to write a complete citation, do your best to provide the information needed to credit your source and lead your readers to it.

General guidelines for listing authors

In APA style, all authors' names are written with the last name first, and initials are used in place of first and middle names. If an author's last name is hyphenated or if an author has a two-part surname, include both names.

Johnson-Sheehan, R.

García Márquez, G.

If the first name is hyphenated, include a hyphen with no spaces between the initials.

Kang, D.-W.

If an author's name has a suffix, such as "Jr.," include it after the initials.

Foreman, G., Jr.

The first element is important because citations in the text refer to it. In-text citations point readers to complete references in an alphabetized reference list.

1. One author   Give the author's last name, followed by a comma, and then give the first and middle initials (if provided in the source), each followed by a period.

Gazzaniga, M. S.

2. Two authors   List each author, last name first. Insert a comma after the initial(s) of the first author, and use an ampersand (&) between the two names.

Bloomberg, M., & Pope, C.

3. Three to twenty authors   List up to twenty authors, each one last name first, followed by any initials. Include a comma after each author and an ampersand (&) before the last author.

Wiegand, I., Seidel, C., & Wolfe, J.

4. Twenty-one or more authors   For twenty-one or more authors, list the first nineteen, followed by an ellipsis mark (. . .) and the last author, without an ampersand (&) before the last author.

Sharon, G., Cruz, N. J., Kang, D.-W., Gandal, M. J., Wang, B., Kim, Y.-M., Zink, E. M., Casey, C. P., Taylor, B. C., Lane, C. J., Bramer, L. M., Isern, N. G., Hoyt, D. W., Noecker, C., Sweredoski, M. J., Moradian, A., Borenstein, E., Jansson, J. K., Knight, R., . . . Mazmanian, S. K.

5. Organization as author   When the author is a corporation, a government agency, or some other organization, begin with the name of the organization.

American Psychiatric Association.

National Highway Traffic Safety Administration.

For works by government agencies, list the most specific organization as the author. For a work by the National Highway Traffic Safety Administration, for example, the NHTSA would be listed as the author, and the U.S. Department of Transportation would be listed as the publisher of the source.

6. Pseudonym or screen name   If you know the writer's actual name, provide it in inverted order, with the screen name or handle following in square brackets.

King, L. [@kingsthings].

If you do not know the writer's actual name, provide the full screen name, not inverted.

Trinity Resists.

7. Author with a one- or two-word name   If the author uses a single name (like "Prince" or "Sophocles") or a two-part name in which the two parts are both essential (like "Snoop Dogg" or "Cardi B"), include that name in the author position.

Plato. (2016). *The republic* (B. Jowett, Trans.). Project Gutenberg. http://www.gutenberg.org/files/1497/1497-h/1497-h.htm (Original work published ca. 380 B.C.E.)

8. Unknown author   Unless the author is listed on the work as "Anonymous," begin the reference list entry with the work's title. For a stand-alone work, put the title in italics.

Atlas of the world. (2019). Oxford University Press.

For a work that is part of a larger whole, put the title in the regular font, with no quotation marks or italics.

Pushed out. (2019, August 24). *The Economist, 432*(9157), 19–20.

9. Author and editor   Include the editor's name, in parentheses, following the title, plus the label "Ed." (for "Editor") or "Eds." (for "Editors").

Sontag, S. (2018). *Debriefing: Collected stories* (B. Taylor, Ed.). Picador.

10. Editor   For an edited work, put the editor's name in the author position, followed by the label "(Ed.)" for "Editor."

Yeh, K.-H. (Ed.). (2019). *Asian indigenous psychologies in the global context*. Palgrave.

If there are multiple editors, use the abbreviation "(Eds.)."

11. Translator

Calasso, R. (2019). *The unnamable present* (R. Dixon, Trans.). Farrar, Straus and Giroux. (Original work published 2017)

12. Editor and translator

Weber, M. (2020). *Charisma and disenchantment: The vocation lectures* (P. Reitter & C. Wellmon, Eds.; D. Searls, Trans.). NYRB Classics. (Original work published 1919)

13. Two or more works by the same author in the same year   Insert lowercase letters following the year in the order in which the sources appear in the reference list ("a" for the first item, "b" for the second item, "c" for the third item, and so on). Works that include only the year (such as books and articles in scholarly journals) precede works that include a year, month, and day (such as articles in newspapers and magazines).

Gladwell, M. (2019a). *Talking to strangers: What we should know about the people we don't know*. Little, Brown and Company.

Gladwell, M. (2019b, January 14). Is marijuana as safe as we think? *The New Yorker*. https://www.newyorker.com/magazine/2019/01/14/is-marijuana-as-safe-as-we-think

If both works use a more specific date, arrange the citations chronologically.

Conover, E. (2019a, June 8). Gold's origins tied to collapsars. *Science News*, *195*(10), 10. https://bit.ly/31JTgKD

Conover, E. (2019b, June 22). Space flames may hold secrets to soot-free fire. *Science News*, *195*(11), 5. https://bit.ly/2p0Xj89

If both works use the year alone or use the same more complete date, then alphabetize the citations by title (ignoring "A," "An," or "The" at the start of a title) before assigning a lowercase letter to each.

Articles and other parts of larger works

If you are using an article from a periodical (journal, magazine, newspaper) or a section from a book or other text-based longer work, use one of the models in this section. (For stand-alone works such as books, audiovisual or multimedia works, or social media, see the sections that follow.) Also refer to the "Title" and "Source" sections of "Elements of APA reference list entries" on pages 10–12.

14. Journal article

Ganegoda, D. B., & Bordia, P. (2019). I can be happy for you, but not all the time: A contingency model of envy and positive empathy in the workplace. *Journal of Applied Psychology, 104*(6), 776–795. https://doi.org/10.1037/apl0000377

Hung, J. (2018). Educational investment and sociopsychological wellbeing among rural Chinese women. *Inquiries Journal, 10*(05). http://www.inquiriesjournal.com/a?id=1736

Le Texier, T. (2019). Debunking the Stanford Prison Experiment. *American Psychologist, 74*(7), 823–839. https://doi.org/10.1037/amp0000401

Notice that "Stanford Prison Experiment" is capitalized in the last example because it is a proper noun.

15. Magazine article

Vlahos, J. (2019, March). Alexa, I want answers. *Wired*, 58–65. https://www.wired.com/story/amazon-alexa-search-for-the-one-perfect-answer/

If the magazine supplies a DOI or uses volume and issue numbers, include that information as well.

Greengard, S. (2019, August). The algorithm that changed quantum machine learning. *Communications of the ACM, 62*(8), 15–17. https://doi.org/10.1145/3339458

If you lack a direct-link URL (for example, if you accessed the magazine through an academic research database) or if you read the article in print, omit the URL.

Koch, C. (2019, October). Is death reversible? *Scientific American, 321*(4), 34–37.

16. Newspaper article   Include a direct-link URL if available.

Daly, J. (2019, August 2). Duquesne's med school plan part of national trend to train more doctors. *Pittsburgh Post-Gazette.* https://www.post-gazette.com/ news/health/2019/08/02/Duquesne-med-school-national-trend-doctors-osteopathic-medicine-pittsburgh/stories/201908010181

If the direct-link URL is lengthy, you can include a shortened form. (See p. 12 for more about using DOIs and URLs in reference list entries.)

Daly, J. (2019, August 2). Duquesne's med school plan part of national trend to train more doctors. *Pittsburgh Post-Gazette.* https://bit.ly/2Vzrm2l

If you accessed the article using a database or read it in print, omit the URL and include the page number (if available) following the newspaper name.

Finucane, M. (2019, September 25). Americans still eating too many low-quality carbs. *The Boston Globe,* B2.

For news from a website such as BBC News, cite the article as you would a web page (see item 26, p. 22).

17. Newsletter article

Bond, G. (2018, Fall). Celebrities as epidemiologists. *American College of Epidemiology Online Member Newsletter.* https://www.acepidemiology.org/ assets/ACE_Newsletter_Fall_2018%20FINAL.pdf

If it will not be clear that you are citing a newsletter, you may include the label "[Newsletter]" following the title.

18. Comment on an online article   In square brackets following the commenter's name (or screen name) and the comment date and title, include the words "Comment on the article" and then the title of the online article in quotation marks. If the comment is untitled, use up to the first twenty words of the comment itself in the title position. (See also item 6, "Pseudonym or screen name," on p. 16.) Provide a direct URL to the comment if one is available. If not, link to the article.

lollyl2. (2019, September 25). My husband works in IT in a major city down South. He is a permanent employee now, but for years [Comment on the article "The Google workers who voted to unionize in Pittsburgh are part of tech's huge contractor workforce"]. *Slate*. https://fyre. it/0RT8HmeL.4

19. Selection in a collection or anthology, or a chapter in an edited book   Include the page numbers for the section following the source title.

Pettigrew, D. (2018). The suppression of cultural memory and identity in Bosnia and Herzegovina. In J. Lindert & A. T. Marsoobian (Eds.), *Multidisciplinary perspectives on genocide and memory* (pp. 187–198). Springer.

20. Abstract   Best practice is to cite the original source, rather than just the abstract of the source. But if you accessed only the abstract, include "[Abstract]" following the article's title.

Brey, E., & Pauker, K. (2019, December). Teachers' nonverbal behaviors influence children's stereotypic beliefs [Abstract]. *Journal of Experimental Child Psychology*, *188*. https://doi.org/10.1016/j.jecp.2019.104671

21. Article with a title in its title   If the internal title is italicized, retain the italics, but set it in sentence case: Capitalize only the first word of the title and subtitle and any proper nouns.

Fernandez, M. E. (2019, July 30). How *Orange is the new black* said goodbye to the Litchfield inmates. *Vulture*. https://www.vulture.com/2019/07/orange-is-the-new-black-character-endings.html

22. Editorial or letter to the editor   Include a label in square brackets following the title to make clear the type of source you are citing.

Gavin Newsom wants to stop rent gouging. Will lawmakers finally stand up for tenants? [Editorial]. (2019, September 4). *Los Angeles Times*. https://lat.ms/2lBlRm1

Doran, K. (2019, October 11). When the homeless look like grandma or grandpa [Letter to the editor]. *The New York Times*. https://nyti.ms/33foDOK

23. Review   After the review's title, include "[Review of the]" plus the type of production being reviewed (book, film), followed by the title of the work being reviewed and the name of the author or director or other major contributor. If the review is untitled, include the bracketed description in the title position.

Douthat, R. (2019, October 14). A hustle gone wrong [Review of the film *Hustlers,* by L. Scafaria, Dir.]. *National Review*, *71*(18), 47.

Hall, W. (2019). [Review of the book *How to change your mind: The new science of psychedelics,* by M. Pollan]. *Addiction*, *114*(10), 1892–1893. https://doi.org/10.1111/add.14702

24. Published interview   The format of the citation depends on the source type in which the interview appears. For an interview published in print, include the interviewer in the "author" position.

Remnick, D. (2019, July 1). Robert Caro reflects on Robert Moses, L.B.J., and his own career in nonfiction. *The New Yorker*. https://bit.ly/2Lukm3X

Typically, the interview subject will be named in the title of a work published in print, but if not, work the interview subject's name into your text in a signal phrase. (To cite a recorded interview, see item 55, "Lecture, speech, address, or recorded interview," p. 30.)

25. Entry in a reference work   Treat an entry in a reference work like a selection in a collection or anthology, or a chapter in an edited book (see item 19, p. 20).

Brue, A. W., & Wilmshurst, L. (2018). Adaptive behavior assessments. In B. B. Frey (Ed.), *The SAGE encyclopedia of educational research, measurement, and evaluation* (pp. 40–44). SAGE Publications. https://doi.org/10.4135/9781506326139.n21

If a source is intended to be updated regularly, include a retrieval date.

Merriam-Webster. (n.d.). Adscititious. In *Merriam-Webster.com dictionary*. Retrieved
    September 5, 2019, from https://www.merriam-webster.com/dictionary/
    adscititious

Since Wikipedia makes archived versions available, you need not include a retrieval date. Instead, include the URL from the "View history" tab for the version you used.

Behaviorism. (2019, October 11). In *Wikipedia*. https://en.wikipedia.org/w/index.
    php?title=Behaviorism&oldid=915544724

26. Web page or document on a website   Many documents published on websites fall into other categories included in this guide and can be cited using models in other sections. For articles in an online newspaper, for example, follow item 16, "Newspaper article" (p. 19), and for an entry in an online dictionary, follow item 25, "Entry in a reference work" (p. 21). Use one of the models below only when your source doesn't fit in any other category. In these items, the website name follows the title unless author and website name are the same.

Albright, A. (2019, July 25). *The global education challenge: Scaling up to tackle
    the learning crisis*. The Brookings Institution. https://www.brookings.edu/
    wp-content/uploads/2019/07/Brookings_Blum_2019_education.pdf

National Institute of Mental Health. (2016, March). *Seasonal affective disorder*.
    National Institutes of Health. https://www.nimh.nih.gov/health/topics/
    seasonal-affective-disorder/index.shtml

BBC News. (2019, October 31). Goats help save Ronald Reagan Presidential Library.
    https://www.bbc.com/news/world-us-canada-50248549

Books and other stand-alone works

27. Basic format for a book   For most books, include the author's name, the year of publication, the title (in sentence case and italics), the name of the publisher (no location needed), and, if accessed online, the book's DOI or direct-link URL.

Treuer, D. (2019). *The heartbeat of Wounded Knee: Native America from 1890 to the present*. Riverhead Books.

Kilby, P. (2019). *The green revolution: Narratives of politics, technology and gender*. Routledge. https://doi.org/10.4324/9780429200823

28. Edition other than the first   Include the edition number, in parentheses, following the book's title; the period follows the edition number.

Dessler, A. E., & Parson, E. A. (2019). *The science and politics of global climate change: A guide to the debate* (3rd ed.). Cambridge University Press.

29. Collection or anthology   Include the name(s) of the editor(s) followed by the abbreviation "Ed." (for "Editor") or "Eds." (for "Editors") in the author position. For a selection in a collection or anthology, or a chapter in an edited book, see item 19 (p. 20).

Lindert, J., & Marsoobian, A. T. (Eds.). (2018). *Multidisciplinary perspectives on genocide and memory*. Springer.

30. Multivolume work (all volumes)

Zeigler-Hill, V., & Shackelford, T. K. (Eds.). (2018). *The SAGE handbook of personality and individual differences* (Vols. I–III). SAGE Publications.

31. Multivolume work (single volume)   If the volume has its own title, insert a colon following the series title and then the volume number, a period, and the title of the volume, all in italics.

Zeigler-Hill, V., & Shackelford, T. K. (Eds.). (2018). *The SAGE handbook of personality and individual differences: Vol. II. Origins of personality and individual differences*. SAGE Publications.

If the volume you used has its own editor, use that name (rather than the name of the series editor) in the author position. If it is untitled, insert the number of the volume you used, in parentheses and in the regular font, following the series title.

32. Book with a title in its title   If the book's title includes another title, neither italicize the internal title nor place it in quotation marks.

Miller, K. (2018). *I'll be there for you: The one about* Friends. Hanover Square Press.

33. Book in a language other than English   If you consulted the book in its original language, put the title, translated into English, in brackets following the title in its original language.

Díaz de Villegas, N. (2019). *De donde son los gusanos: Crónica de un regreso a Cuba después de 37 años de exilio* [Where the worms are: Chronicle of a return to Cuba after 37 years of exile]. Vintage Español.

34. Republished book   Include the original publication date following the citation. (See also item 13, "Work available in multiple versions," in the in-text citation section, p. 6.)

Fremlin, C. (2017). *The hours before dawn*. Dover Publications. (Original work published 1958)

35. Sacred or classical text   Cite sacred and classical texts like books. Sacred texts typically do not list an author, but you should give the title of the edition you used, the year it was published, the translator's name (if any), and any other source information available for the version you used. For an annotated version, include the editor in the author position. If an original date is known, include it at the end of the citation; if the date is approximate, include "ca." (for "circa"). Include "B.C.E." (for "before the Christian era") for ancient texts.

New International Version Bible. (2011). Biblica. https://www.biblica.com/bible/ (Original work published 1978)

Homer. (2018). *The odyssey* (E. Wilson, Trans.). W. W. Norton & Company. (Original work published ca. 675–725 B.C.E.)

Aurelius, M. (1994). *The meditations* (G. Long, Trans.). The Internet Classics Archive. http://classics.mit.edu/Antoninus/meditations.html (Original work published ca. 167)

36. Government document   If no author is listed, include the department that produced the document in the author position. Any broader organization can be included as the publisher of the document. If a specific report number is provided, include it after the title.

National Park Service. (2019, April 11). *Travel where women made history: Ordinary and extraordinary places of American women*. U.S. Department of the Interior. https://www.nps.gov/subjects/travelwomenshistory/index.htm

Berchick, E. R., Barnett, J. C., & Upton, R. D. (2019, September 10). *Health insurance coverage in the United States: 2018* (Report No. P60-267). U.S. Census Bureau. https://www.census.gov/library/publications/2019/demo/p60-267.html

37. Report from a private organization

Ford Foundation International Fellowships Program. (2019). *Leveraging higher education to promote social justice: Evidence from the IFP alumni tracking study*. https://p.widencdn.net/kei61u/IFP-Alumni-Tracking-Study-Report-5

38. Brochure or fact sheet

National Council of State Boards of Nursing. (2018). *A nurse manager's guide to substance use disorder in nursing* [Brochure].

World Health Organization. (2019, July 15). *Immunization coverage* [Fact sheet]. https://www.who.int/news-room/fact-sheets/detail/immunization-coverage

39. Press release

New York University. (2019, September 5). *NYU Oral Cancer Center awarded $2.5 million NIH grant to study cancer pain* [Press release]. https://www.nyu.edu/about/news-publications/news/2019/september/nyu-oral-cancer-center-awarded--2-5-million-nih-grant-to-study-c.html

40. Website Include a citation to an entire website only if you borrow ideas or information from its home page. (If you merely refer to a website in your paper, without discussing any specific information or ideas, you do not need to include a citation to that website in your reference list.) If you retrieved information that is subject to change, also include the date you accessed the source.

U.S. debt clock. Retrieved October 21, 2019, from https://www.usdebtclock.org/

Multimedia sources

List the person or people most responsible for an audiovisual or multimedia work in the author position, with a label (in parentheses) to clarify their role. Who is "most responsible" depends in large part on the source type: For movies, include the director; for a streaming video, include the person who uploaded it; for a photograph or work of art, include the photographer or artist; for TV or podcast episodes, include the writer and director or the episode host.

Do not include information about how you experienced the material—in a movie theater, on broadcast television, or on a streaming service—unless you watched or listened to a special version, such as a director's cut. This information can be included in square brackets following the title or combined with other bracketed information already included after the title.

41. Blog post   Treat a blog post as you would an article in a magazine or newspaper (items 15–16, pp. 18–19).

Fister, B. (2019, February 14). Information literacy's third wave. *Library Babel Fish.* https://www.insidehighered.com/blogs/library-babel-fish/information-literacy%E2%80%99s-third-wave

42. Comment on a blog post   Treat a comment on a blog post as you would a comment on an online article (see item 18, p. 20).

Mollie F. (2019, February 14). It's a daunting task, isn't it? Last year, I got a course on Scholarly Communication and Information Literacy approved for [Comment on the blog post "Information literacy's third wave"]. *Library Babel Fish.* https://disq.us/p/1zr92uc

43. Podcast   If you merely mention the podcast's name in your text, you need not cite it in your reference list. If you discuss characteristics of the podcast as a whole, however, include an entry.

Boilen, B. (Host). (2008–present). *Tiny desk concerts* [Video podcast]. NPR. https://www.npr.org/series/tiny-desk-concerts/

Abumrad, J., & Krulwich, R. (Hosts). (2002–present). *Radiolab* [Audio podcast]. WNYC Studios. https://www.wnycstudios.org/podcasts/radiolab/podcasts

44. Episode of a podcast   If the episodes are numbered, include the podcast number following the title, in parentheses. If the host of an individual episode differs from the host(s) of the podcast in general, put the episode host's name in the author position, and include the series host(s) in the source information.

West, S. (Host). (2018, July 27). Logical positivism (No. 120) [Audio podcast episode]. In *Philosophize this!* https://philosophizethis.org/logical-positivists/

Longoria, J. (Host & Producer). (2019, April 19). Americanish [Audio podcast episode]. In J. Abumrad & R. Krulwich (Hosts), *Radiolab*. WNYC Studios. https://www.wnycstudios.org/podcasts/radiolab/articles/americanish

45. Online video or audio   Think of the author of an online video or audio file as the person or organization that posted it. For a TED Talk, for example, the presenter is the author if the video was accessed on the TED site. However, if the TED Talk was accessed on YouTube, then TED becomes the author because the TED organization posted the video.

Wray, B. (2019, May). *How climate change affects your mental health* [Video]. TED Conferences. https://www.ted.com/talks/britt_wray_how_climate_change_affects_your_mental_health

TED. (2019, September 20). *Britt Wray: How climate change affects your mental health* [Video]. YouTube. https://www.youtube.com/watch?v=IlDkCEvsYw

When deciding whether to italicize the title of the video or audio file, consider whether it is part of a series (regular font) or a standalone item (italics).

BBC. (2018, November 19). Why do bad managers flourish? [Audio]. In *Business Matters*. https://www.bbc.co.uk/programmes/p06s8752

The New York Times. (2018, January 9). *Taking a knee and taking down a monument* [Video]. YouTube. https://www.youtube.com/watch?v=qY34DQCdUvQ

46. Transcript of an online video or audio file

Gopnik, A. (2019, July 10). *A separate kind of intelligence* [Video transcript]. Edge.
    https://www.edge.org/conversation/alison_gopnik-a-separate-kind-of-intelligence

Glass, I. (2019, August 23). Ten sessions (No. 682) [Audio podcast episode
    transcript]. In *This American life*. WBEZ. https://www.thisamericanlife.
    org/682/transcript

47. Film   Include the production company after the title. Separate multiple production companies with semicolons.

Peele, J. (Director). (2017). *Get out* [Film]. Universal Pictures.

Hitchcock, A. (Director). (1959). *The essentials collection: North by northwest*
    [Film; five-disc special ed. on DVD]. Metro-Goldwyn-Mayer; Universal Pictures
    Home Entertainment.

48. Television or radio series

Waller-Bridge, P., Williams, H., & Williams, J. (Executive Producers). (2016–2019).
    Fleabag. Two Brothers Pictures; BBC.

49. Episode from a television or radio series

Waller-Bridge, P. (Writer), & Bradbeer, H. (Director). (2019, March 18). The
    provocative request (Season 2, Episode 3) [TV series episode]. In P. Waller-
    Bridge, H. Williams, & J. Williams (Executive Producers), *Fleabag*. Two
    Brothers Pictures; BBC.

50. Work of art in a museum   Include information about the museum following the artwork's title. If a photograph of the image is available on the museum's website, include the direct-link URL.

O'Keeffe, G. (1931). *Cow's skull: Red, white, and blue* [Painting]. Metropolitan
    Museum of Art, New York, NY, United States. https://www.metmuseum.org/
    art/collection/search/488694

Helmet mask (kakaparaga) [Artifact]. (ca. late 19th century). Museum of Fine Arts,
    Boston, MA, United States.

51. Photograph   For a photograph that is available outside of a museum's collection, include the title of the photograph (if any), followed by the label "Photograph" in brackets. If the photograph is untitled, include a bracketed description that includes the word "photograph" in the title position. In the source position, include the name of the site you used to access the photograph.

Browne, M. (1963). *The burning monk* [Photograph]. Time. http://100photos.time.com/photos/malcolm-browne-burning-monk

Liittschwager, D. (2019). [Photograph series of octopuses]. National Geographic. https://www.nationalgeographic.com/animals/2019/10/pet-octopuses-are-a-problem/#/01-pet-octopus-trade-nationalgeographic_2474095.jpg

52. Map

Desjardins, J. (2017, November 17). *Walmart nation: Mapping the largest employers in the U.S.* [Map]. Visual Capitalist. https://www.visualcapitalist.com/walmart-nation-mapping-largest-employers-u-s/

53. Advertisement   Use the model for the source in which the advertisement appears.

America's Biopharmaceutical Companies [Advertisement]. (2018, September). *The Atlantic, 322*(2), 2.

Centers for Disease Control and Prevention. (n.d.). *A tip from a former smoker: Beatrice* [Advertisement]. U.S. Department of Health and Human Services. https://www.cdc.gov/tobacco/campaign/tips/resources/ads/pdf-print-ads/beatrices-tip-print-ad-7x10.pdf

54. Music recording   For classical works, put the composer in the author position, and provide information about the performer in brackets after the title. For popular works, put the performer in the author position. Include multiple record labels separated by semicolons.

Nielsen, C. (2014). *Carl Nielsen: Symphonies 1 & 4* [Album recorded by New York Philharmonic Orchestra]. Dacapo Records. (Original work published 1892–1916)

Carlile, B. (2018). *By the way, I forgive you* [Album]. Low Country Sound; Elektra.

Carlile, B. (2018). The mother [Song]. On *By the way, I forgive you*. Low Country Sound; Elektra.

55. Lecture, speech, address, or recorded interview

Grigas, A. (2019, October 8). *The new geopolitics of energy* [Address]. Freeman Spogli Institute for International Studies, Stanford University, Stanford, CA, United States.

Parrado, N. (2011, March 27). *Nando Parrado, plane crash survivor* [Interview with C. Gracie; audio file]. The Interview Archive; BBC World Service. https://www.bbc.co.uk/programmes/p00fhjnb

For an interview in an archive, put the person interviewed in the author position.

56. Paper or poster presented at a conference   Include all those involved with the conference presentation, even if only one person was actually at the conference; the full dates of the conference or meeting (not just the presentation date); the title of the presentation or poster, followed by a label (in brackets) stating the nature of the presentation (as described in conference materials); and the name and location of the conference. If there is a link to the presentation or poster, include it at the end of the reference list entry.

Vasylets, O. (2019, April 10–13). *Memory accuracy in bilinguals depends on the valence of the emotional event* [Paper presentation]. XIV International Symposium of Psycholinguistics, Tarragona, Spain. https://psico.fcep.urv.cat/projectes/gip/files/isp2019.pdf

Wood, M. (2019, January 3–6). *The effects of an adult development course on students' perceptions of aging* [Poster session]. Forty-First Annual National Institute on the Teaching of Psychology, St. Pete Beach, FL, United States. https://nitop.org/resources/Documents/2019%20Poster%20Session%20II.pdf

If you are citing a paper delivered at a conference but published in a journal, cite the source as you would a journal article (item 14, p. 18); if you are citing a paper published in a collection of conference presentations, cite the source as you would a selection in a collection or anthology, or a chapter in an edited book (item 19, p. 20).

57. Video game

ConcernedApe. (2016). *Stardew Valley* [Video game]. Chucklefish.

58. Mobile app If you merely mention the app, include an in-text citation only; include a reference list entry only if you discuss the app in a significant way.

Google LLC. (2019). *Google earth* (Version 9.3.3) [Mobile app]. App Store. https:// apps.apple.com/us/app/google-earth/id293622097

59. Presentation slides If the presentation slide is inaccessible to your readers, cite it only in the text of your paper.

Centers for Disease Control and Prevention. (2019, April 16). *Building local response capacity to protect families from emerging health threats* [Presentation slides]. CDC Stacks. https://stacks.cdc.gov/view/cdc/77687

Social media sources

If a social media source is not accessible to all readers, cite the post in the text of your paper only. For any social media sources that are accessible to your readers, use the author's real name, if given, followed by the pseudonym or screen name in brackets, exactly as in the source. If you know only the screen name, begin with that name without brackets. If the posting is undated, use "n.d." in parentheses. If untitled, include up to the first 20 words of the post or caption, or use a description of the post in square brackets. Include any emojis, hashtags, and links from the post if possible (each counts as one word), and keep unconventional spelling or capitalization as is. If you cannot use an actual emoji (😊), then include its name in square brackets ("[kissing face emoji]") instead. Describe images, or recordings, and the type of post in brackets following the title. Include an access date only if the post is not archived or if the content is likely to change.

60. Profile

National Science Foundation [@NSF]. (n.d.). *Tweets* [Twitter profile]. Twitter.
    Retrieved October 15, 2019, from https://twitter.com/NSF

61. Facebook post

Georgia Aquarium. (2019, October 10). *Meet the bigfin reef squid* [Video]. Facebook.
    https://www.facebook.com/GeorgiaAquarium/videos/2471961729567512/

Georgia Aquarium. (2019, June 25). *True love ❤ Charlie and Lizzy are a bonded pair
    of African penguins who have been together for more than* [Image attached]
    [Status update]. Facebook. https://www.facebook.com/GeorgiaAquarium/
    photos/a.163898398123/10156900637543124/?type=3&theater

62. Tweet

Schiller, Caitlin [@caitlinschiller]. (2019, September 26). *Season 6 of* Simplify *is
    here! Today we launch with the one and only @susancain, author of* Quiet
    [Thumbnail with link attached] [Tweet]. Twitter. http://twitter.com/
    caitlinschiller/status/1177214094191026176

63. Instagram post or highlight

Smithsonian [@smithsonian]. (2019, October 7). *You're looking at a ureilite
    meteorite under a microscope. When illuminated with polarized light, they
    appear in dazzling colors, influenced* [Photograph]. Instagram. https://www.
    instagram.com/p/B3VI27yHLQG/

Smithsonian [@smithsonian]. (n.d.). *#Apollo50* [Highlight]. Instagram.
    Retrieved October 15, 2019, from https://www.instagram.com/stories/
    highlights/17902787752343364/

64. Online forum post

ScienceModerator. (2018, November 16). *Science discussion: We are researchers
    working with some of the largest and most innovative companies using DNA to
    help people* [Online forum post]. Reddit. https://www.reddit.com/r/science/
    comments/9xlnm2/science_discussion_we_are_researchers_working/

Other sources

65. Data set or graphic representation of data (graph, chart, table)

Reid, L. (2019). *Smarter homes: Experiences of living in low carbon homes 2013–2018* [Data set]. UK Data Service. http://doi.org/10.5255/UKDA-SN-853485

Pew Research Center. (2018, November 15). *U.S. public is closely divided about overall health risk from food additives* [Chart]. https://www.pewinternet.org/2018/11/19/public-perspectives-on-food-risks/ps_2018-11-19_food_0-01/

66. Legal source   The title of a court case is not italicized in the reference list, though it is italicized in the in-text citation.

Sweatt v. Painter, 339 U.S. 629 (1950). http://www.law.cornell.edu/supct/html/historics/USSC_CR_0339_0629_ZS.html

67. Personal communications   Omit personal communications — letters, text messages, or email messages you have received, lecture notes that you took or that are posted only on a server your readers cannot access, and so on — from your reference list. Describe them only in the text of your paper. (See item 17 in the section on in-text citations, p. 8.)

Formatting student papers in APA style

The following guidelines for formatting a student paper and preparing a reference list are consistent with advice given in the *Publication Manual of the American Psychological Association*, 7th ed. (2020). The excerpts from a sample student paper (p. 38) provide a model.

Margins and fonts   Use one-inch margins on all sides (the default setting in most word processing programs). Use a 10- to 12-point font that is accessible to readers, such as Arial, Times New Roman, or Calibri. Some instructors may have their own font requirements. With the exception of any footnotes, which should be set in 10-point type, set the whole paper in the same font size.

Indents For the text of the paper, use paragraph indents of one-half inch. Quotations of forty or more words should be indented one-half inch from the left margin, but they do not use a paragraph indent unless the quotation is more than one paragraph long.

Footnotes (or endnotes) Footnotes appear at the bottom of the page on which they are called out, and endnotes are gathered up at the end of the paper, following the reference list. Footnotes typically add information that is relevant and informative but that does not fit into the body of the essay. If you need to include them, set them single-spaced in a 10-point font, using the footnote function in your word processor to number them consecutively with arabic numbers (1, 2, 3, and so on).

Line spacing Except for any footnotes or tables, double-space your whole paper, including the title page and reference list. Set footnotes single-spaced, and set tables single-spaced, one-and-a-half-spaced, or double-spaced, depending on what is easiest to read and understand.

Page numbering Number all pages in the upper right-hand corner, one-half inch from the top of the page and one inch from the right margin. The title page is page 1. Do not include the title or your name at the top of each page, unless your instructor requires it.

Headings Not all papers need headings, but if you are writing a long or complex paper and headings would help guide your reader, insert them. All headings use title case: Capitalize the first and last words, all other significant words, and any words of four or more letters.

First-Level Heading (centered, boldface)

Second-Level Heading (left-aligned, boldface)

Third-Level Heading (left-aligned, boldface, italics)

    Fourth-Level Heading. (indent, boldface, period at end; text runs in)

    Fifth-Level Heading. (indent, boldface, italics, period at end; text runs in)

Title page   Unless your instructor directs you otherwise, your title page should include the following information, centered on the page:

- the title of the paper in boldface type, three or four double-spaced lines from the top margin
- your name and the names of any coauthors, one blank double-spaced line below the title
- your school and the department in which the course is offered
- the course number and name (using the format shown in the catalog or on other school sites)
- your instructor's name (check to see how your instructor would like to be addressed: for example, as "Professor" or "Dr.")
- the assignment due date (in the date format of the country you are in)

Additional sections for professional papers

The following elements are not required for student papers; they are typical requirements for professional papers intended for publication. Your instructor may request that you use some or all of these elements (an abstract for a long or complex paper, for instance). If so, these guidelines will help you format those sections.

Author note   Set an author note (titled "Author Note" in boldface font) at the bottom of the title page. In the first paragraph, include any acknowledgments (such as thanks for assistance) or disclosures (such as of conflicts of interest); in the second paragraph, include your contact information. Begin each paragraph at the left margin, with the first line indented one-half inch.

Abstract   An abstract is a one-paragraph summary (fewer than 250 words) of the main points of the paper. If your instructor requests one, use the following format:

- Place the abstract on its own page, after the title page.
- Center the heading "Abstract" (in boldface type) at the top of the page.

- Start the abstract itself one double-spaced line below the heading.
- Do not indent the first line of the paragraph.

Keywords Keywords are terms for indexing the paper in databases. If your instructor asks you to supply them, they should be typed one double-spaced line below the abstract. Begin the line with *"Keywords:"* (in italics), indented one-half inch; then type the keywords in lowercase letters (except for proper nouns), separated by commas, and with no period at the end of the list.

Running heads On every page of the paper, including the title page, type the title of the paper (shortened to no more than 50 characters), flush with the left margin in all capital letters. On the same line, flush with the right margin, type the page number. Number all pages, including the title page.

Preparing the reference list

Begin the reference list on a new page at the end of the paper. Center the heading "References" one inch from the top of the page, and set it in boldface type. Double-space the entire reference list.

Alphabetizing the list Alphabetize the reference list by the authors' (or editors') last names; if a work has no author or editor, alphabetize it by the first word of the title other than "A," "An," or "The."

   If you used more than one work by the same author, order those works by date, from earliest to latest. If you used more than one work by the same author in the same year, see item 9 in the in-text citation section (p. 5) and item 13 in the reference list section (p. 17).

Formatting the entries Start the first line of each entry at the left margin; indent lines after the first one-half inch (a "hanging indent"). Use your word processor settings to make the hanging indent.

DOIs and URLs   If a DOI or URL is lengthy, you can include a shortened form by using a site like shortdoi.org or bitly.com. Permalinks (provided by some publications, such as *The New York Times*) are often short, so use those if available. Do not manually add line breaks to URLs or DOIs. If your word processor inserts line breaks automatically or moves a DOI or URL to its own line, you can accept that formatting.

Excerpts from a sample student paper in APA style

Title page

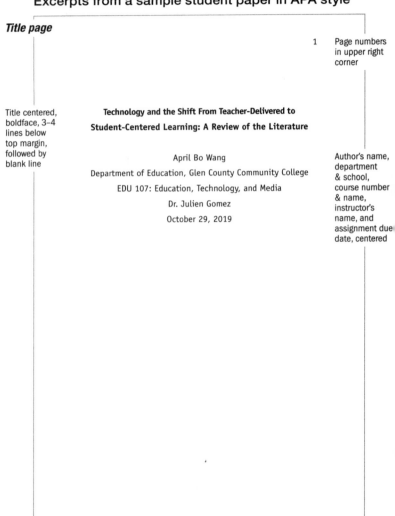

Title centered, boldface, 3–4 lines below top margin, followed by blank line

1   Page numbers in upper right corner

Technology and the Shift From Teacher-Delivered to Student-Centered Learning: A Review of the Literature

April Bo Wang
Department of Education, Glen County Community College
EDU 107: Education, Technology, and Media
Dr. Julien Gomez
October 29, 2019

Author's name, department & school, course number & name, instructor's name, and assignment due date, centered

Marginal annotations indicate APA-style formatting.

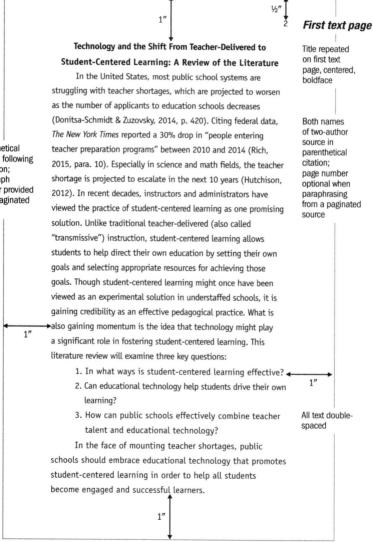

½″
2

First text page

½″ / 1″

Technology and the Shift From Teacher-Delivered to Student-Centered Learning: A Review of the Literature

Title repeated on first text page, centered, boldface

In the United States, most public school systems are struggling with teacher shortages, which are projected to worsen as the number of applicants to education schools decreases (Donitsa-Schmidt & Zuzovsky, 2014, p. 420). Citing federal data, *The New York Times* reported a 30% drop in "people entering teacher preparation programs" between 2010 and 2014 (Rich, 2015, para. 10). Especially in science and math fields, the teacher shortage is projected to escalate in the next 10 years (Hutchison, 2012). In recent decades, instructors and administrators have viewed the practice of student-centered learning as one promising solution. Unlike traditional teacher-delivered (also called "transmissive") instruction, student-centered learning allows students to help direct their own education by setting their own goals and selecting appropriate resources for achieving those goals. Though student-centered learning might once have been viewed as an experimental solution in understaffed schools, it is gaining credibility as an effective pedagogical practice. What is also gaining momentum is the idea that technology might play a significant role in fostering student-centered learning. This literature review will examine three key questions:

1. In what ways is student-centered learning effective?
2. Can educational technology help students drive their own learning?
3. How can public schools effectively combine teacher talent and educational technology?

In the face of mounting teacher shortages, public schools should embrace educational technology that promotes student-centered learning in order to help all students become engaged and successful learners.

Parenthetical citation following quotation; paragraph number provided for unpaginated source

Both names of two-author source in parenthetical citation; page number optional when paraphrasing from a paginated source

1″

All text double-spaced

1″

3

Heading centered
and boldface

Signal phrase
followed by year
in parentheses

Shortened
section heading
(in quotation
marks) for direct
quotation from
unpaginated
source

Callout for table
that appears on
next page

Page number
provided for
quotation from
paginated
source

In What Ways Is Student-Centered Learning Effective?

According to the International Society for Technology in Education (2016), "Student-centered learning moves students from passive receivers of information to active participants in their own discovery process. What students learn, how they learn it, and how their learning is assessed are all driven by each individual student's needs and abilities" ("What Is It" section). The results of student-centered learning have been positive, not only for academic achievement but also for student self-esteem. In this model of instruction, the teacher acts as a facilitator, and the students actively participate in the process of learning and teaching. With guidance, students decide on the learning goals most pertinent to themselves, they devise a learning plan that will most likely help them achieve those goals, they direct themselves in carrying out that learning plan, and they assess how much they learned (Çubukçu, 2012). The major differences between student-centered learning and instructor-centered learning are summarized in Table 1.

Bell (2010) has argued that the chief benefit of student-centered learning is that it can connect students with "real-world tasks" (p. 42), thus making learning more engaging as well as more comprehensive. For example, Bell observed a group of middle-school students who wanted to build a social justice monument for their school. They researched social justice issues, selected several to focus on, and then designed a three-dimensional playground to represent those issues. In doing so, they achieved learning goals in the areas of social studies, physics, and mathematics and practiced research and teamwork.

4

Table 1

Comparison of Two Approaches to Teaching and Learning

Table left-aligned, number boldface, title italic

Teaching and learning period	Instructor-centered approach	Student-centered approach
Before class	• Instructor prepares a lecture/instruction on a new topic. • Students complete homework on the previous topic.	• Students read and practice new concepts, and prepare questions ahead of class. • Instructor views student questions and practice and identifies learning opportunities.
During class	• Instructor delivers new material in a lecture or prepared discussion. • Students—unprepared—listen, watch, take notes, and try to follow along with the new material.	• Students lead discussions or practice applying the concepts or skills in an active environment. • Instructor answers student questions and provides immediate feedback.
After class	• Instructor grades homework and gives feedback about the previous lesson. • Students work independently to practice or apply the new concepts.	• Students apply the concepts/skills to more complex tasks, individually and in groups. • Instructor posts additional resources to help students.

Column heads centered

Note. Adapted from *The Flipped Class Demystified*, by New York University, n.d. (https://www.nyu.edu/faculty/teaching-and-learning-resources/instructional-technology-support/instructional-design-assessment/flipped-classes/the-flipped-class-demystified.html).

Note providing source of information in table

6

As the teacher shortage has intensified, educational technology has become tailored to student needs and more affordable. Backpacks that charge electronic devices and apps that create audiovisual flash cards are just two of the more recent innovations. According to Svokos (2015), College and Education Fellow for *The Huffington Post*, some educational technology entertains students while supporting student-centered learning:

> GlassLab, a nonprofit that was launched with grants from the Bill & Melinda Gates and MacArthur Foundations, creates educational games that are now being used in more than 6,000 classrooms across the country. Some of the company's games are education versions of existing ones—for example, its first release was SimCity EDU— while others are originals. Teachers get realtime updates on students' progress as well as suggestions on what subjects they need to spend more time perfecting.
>
> (5. Educational Games section)

Many of the companies behind these products offer discounts to schools where such devices are widely used.

Conclusion

Not only has student-centered learning proved effective in improving student academic and developmental outcomes, but it can also synchronize with technological learning for widespread adaptability across schools. Because it relies on student direction rather than an established curriculum, student-centered learning supported by educational technology can adapt to the different needs of individual students and a variety of learning environments—urban and rural, well funded and underfunded. Similarly, when student-centered learning relies on technology rather than a corps of uniformly trained teachers, it holds promise for schools that would otherwise suffer from a lack of human or financial resources.

Block quotation (forty or more words) set off with ½" indent; no quotation marks

Quotation location provided after period

Conclusion, with heading centered, boldface

Reference list

7

Reference list begins on new page

References heading centered, boldface

First line of each entry at left margin; all other lines indented ½"

References ordered alphabetically by author name, or by title, if no author listed

Shortened URL created and provided for complex URL

References

Bell, S. (2010). Project-based learning for the 21st century: Skills for the future. *The Clearing House, 83*(2), 39–43.

Çubukçu, Z. (2012). Teachers' evaluation of student-centered learning environments. *Education, 133*(1), 49–66.

Donitsa-Schmidt, S., & Zuzovsky, R. (2014). Teacher supply and demand: The school level perspective. *American Journal of Educational Research, 2*(6), 420–429. https://doi.org/10.12691/education-2-6-14

Friedlaender, D., Burns, D., Lewis-Charp, H., Cook-Harvey, C. M., & Darling-Hammond, L. (2014). *Student-centered schools: Closing the opportunity gap* [Research brief]. Stanford Center for Opportunity Policy in Education. https://edpolicy.stanford.edu/sites/default/files/scope-pub-student-centered-research-brief.pdf

Hutchison, L. F. (2012). Addressing the STEM teacher shortage in American schools: Ways to recruit and retain effective STEM teachers. *Action in Teacher Education, 34*(5/6), 541–550. https://doi.org/10.1080/01626620.2012.729483

International Society for Technology in Education. (2016). *Student-centered learning*. https://id.iste.org/connected/standards/essential-conditions/

Rich, M. (2015, August 9). Teacher shortages spur a nationwide hiring scramble (credentials optional). *The New York Times*. https://nyti.ms/1WaaV7a

Svokos, A. (2015, May 7). 5 innovations from the past decade that aim to change the American classroom. *Huffington Post*. https://bit.ly/33FjRcW

DOI included when available

All authors' names listed, up to twenty authors

Organization as author